ALBERT
EINSTEIN

RELATIVITY ROCK STAR

ALBERT EINSTEIN

RELATIVITY ROCK STAR

MATT DOEDEN

LERNER PUBLICATIONS ◆ MINNEAPOLIS

Lerner Publications Company
An imprint of Lerner Publishing Group, Inc.
241 First Avenue North
Minneapolis, MN 55401 USA

For reading levels and more information, look up this title at www.lernerbooks.com.

Image credits: ETH-Bibliothek Zürich, Bildarchiv, pp. 2, 10, 16, 17; Wikimedia Commons (public domain), pp. 6, 28; Heritage Images/Hulton Archive/Getty Images, p. 8; Sueddeutsche Zeitung Photo/Alamy Stock Photo, p. 9; Bridgeman Images, p. 11; travellinglight/iStock/Getty Images, p. 13; Christie's/Wikimedia Commons (public domain), p. 14; The Granger Collection, New York, p. 18; Science & Society Picture Library/Getty Images, p. 19 (right); Richard Baker/Corbis News/ Getty Images, p. 20; ESA–C.Carreau, p. 23; ESO/Landessternwarte Heidelberg-Königstuhl/ F. W. Dyson, A. S. Eddington, & C. Davidson (CC BY 4.0), p. 24; Pictorial Press Ltd/Alamy Stock Photo, p. 25; Library of Congress, pp. 26, 38; Event Horizon Telescope Collaboration (CC BY 3.0), p. 27; Apic/Hulton Archive/Getty Images, p. 30; Hulton-Deutsch Collection/Corbis Historical/ Getty Images, p. 31; Time Life Pictures/Getty Images, p. 32; University of New Hampshire/Gado/ Getty Images, p. 33; Topical Press Agency/Hulton Archive/Getty Images, p. 34; Courtesy of the Los Alamos National Laboratory Archives, p. 35; Bettmann/Getty Images, pp. 36, 40; Keystone/ Hulton Archive/Getty Images, p. 37; Ann Ronan Pictures/Print Collector/Hulton Archive/Getty Images, p. 39. Cover: Fred Stein Archive/Archive Photos/Getty Images.

Main body text set in Rotis Serif Std 55 Regular.
Typeface provided by Adobe Systems.

Library of Congress Cataloging-in-Publication Data

Names: Doeden, Matt, author.
Title: Albert Einstein : relativity rock star / Matt Doeden.
Other titles: Gateway biographies (Lerner Publications Company)
Description: Minneapolis : Lerner Publications, [2020] | Series: Gateway biographies | Includes
  bibliographical references and index. | Audience: Ages 9–14. | Audience: Grades 4–6. |
  Summary: "Albert Einstein rewrote the rules of physics and changed how scientists see space
  and time forever. Learn how a boy who had trouble in school became one of history's most
  renowned scientists"– Provided by publisher.
Identifiers: LCCN 2019028064 (print) | LCCN 2019028065 (ebook) | ISBN 9781541577435
  (hardcover) | ISBN 9781541588851 (paperback) | ISBN 9781541583030 (ebook)
Subjects: LCSH: Einstein, Albert, 1879-1955–Juvenile literature. | Physicists–Biography–
  Juvenile literature. | Relativity (Physics)–History–Juvenile literature.
Classification: LCC QC16.E5 D64 2020 (print) | LCC QC16.E5 (ebook) | DDC 530.092 [B]–dc23

LC record available at https://lccn.loc.gov/2019028064
LC ebook record available at https://lccn.loc.gov/2019028065

Manufactured in the United States of America
1-46766-47757-9/4/2019

CONTENTS

Albert Einstein during a lecture in Vienna in 1921

In 1905 twenty-five-year-old Albert Einstein sat in a small patent office in Bern, Switzerland. Patent applications lay scattered across the desk in front of him. Inventors sent in the applications to ensure others would not copy their work. Diagrams and blueprints explained their various inventions. Einstein looked over the applications, making sure each invention was truly new.

It was a tedious job. Einstein did not enjoy it. As he looked at invention after invention, his mind was often elsewhere. He thought about the universe and how it worked. He imagined speeding alongside a beam of light. He wondered what the light would look like and how the universe would change around him. In his mind, he dove deeper and deeper into the question. Occasionally, he scrawled his thoughts on scratch paper.

At the time, research into physics was booming. Researchers were learning more and more about light, matter, and energy. They expanded upon classical theories, making them increasingly detailed. A greater

Albert Einstein working at the Swiss patent office in Bern, 1905

understanding of how the universe works seemed just on the horizon.

Then came Einstein. He was an unknown patent clerk who had been unable to find a teaching job at any university. He had no access to scientific tools or a laboratory. Using only his mind, Einstein had delved more deeply into the mysteries of light, matter, and energy than anyone before. He had reached a conclusion: the accepted physics theories of his time were wrong.

That year Einstein published a flurry of scientific papers that turned the science world upside down. He showed a universe that was relative. Time behaved differently based on an object's acceleration. Light was both a wave and a group of particles. Not only were energy and mass made of the same stuff, but they could convert back and forth, one becoming the other.

Long-held beliefs about the universe fell like dominoes. Einstein revealed truths about a universe that was stranger than anyone had imagined.

An Unusual Child

Albert Einstein was born on March 14, 1879, in Ulm, in what was then the German Empire. He was his parents' first child. His father, Hermann Einstein, ran his own electrical workshop. His mother, Pauline Einstein, cared for Albert, and later for his younger sister, Maria.

Albert's parents, Pauline and Hermann Einstein

Einstein's business struggled. When Albert was around a year old, Einstein shut it down and moved the family to Munich. There, he opened a new workshop, and his business flourished. The family was never wealthy, but Einstein's electrical business kept them comfortable.

Meanwhile, Albert was proving to be an unusual child. Most children begin to speak at around one year old and use only a few words at a time. Albert didn't start speaking until he was two years old. When he did finally speak, he spoke in full sentences. He was careful with his

Albert and his sister, Maria, in 1885

Albert when he was fourteen

words, often saying them softly to himself before sharing them aloud. The habit left him constantly repeating himself, even into adulthood.

Einstein later explained that words came slowly to him because he thought differently than everyone else. "I very rarely think in words at all," he later explained. "A thought comes, and I may try to express it in words afterwards."

Albert's speech wasn't the only thing that set him apart. He preferred to play alone, often with blocks or puzzles. He had a terrible temper. He was prone to angry outbursts, both at adults and at other children, including his sister. Yet in other ways, Albert showed patience remarkable for a child. He built massive houses of cards and showed no anger or frustration when his creations crumbled. Above all, Albert was curious. Any new toy his parents brought home received his undivided attention. He would stick with a toy or game until he learned how it worked and mastered it.

Though the Einstein family had Jewish roots, they were nonobservant Jews. They didn't follow Jewish laws or traditions. The family lived in a neighborhood dominated by Roman Catholic families, and starting at the age of five, Albert attended a Catholic school. The teachers there were strict. They wanted students to memorize facts and did little to encourage free thought. The teaching style did not suit Albert, and he found school difficult. He learned slowly, was often distracted, and had trouble making friends. One of his teachers even declared that Albert would never amount to anything.

A Passion for Music

Music was one of Einstein's earliest passions. Even while he struggled in school, he excelled in music. Einstein took violin lessons and showed some talent for the instrument. As a child, he composed his own songs. Music calmed him and helped him focus. He said later in life that had he not become a scientist, he might have been a musician.

A Curious Mind

As an adult, Einstein identified two events that shaped the direction of his life. First, when Albert was five years old, his father brought him a compass. The tool fascinated Albert. No matter how he held it or turned it, the compass's needle always pointed north. He realized that some unseen force must have been acting on the needle. The idea of invisible forces operating on the universe filled him with awe.

The second event occurred when Albert was twelve years old. He came across a book on geometry. Reading the book helped to ignite a deep interest in science and mathematics.

Until then Albert had been very religious, despite his parents' secular life. He believed in God and wanted to please God. He read

Because the Earth itself is magnetic, it moves the magnet within a compass to always point north.

religious texts and even composed songs to God. But as Albert pursued his scientific interests, he found science clashing with his religious beliefs. To him, there were two possibilities: either physical laws governed the universe or God did. He was unable to reconcile the two ideas.

Eventually, Albert dismissed organized religion. It no longer had a place in his life. His disillusionment with religion sparked a deep mistrust of authority in Albert.

By the time Albert was sixteen, he was already deeply interested in the science he would study as an adult.

This mistrust stayed with him for the rest of his life.

From then on, Albert focused on the universe and its workings. When he was sixteen, a tutor introduced him to a series of books on physical science. In one of them, the author imagined what it would be like to travel along an electrical wire. The idea stuck with Albert. He wondered what a beam of light might look like and how quickly it might travel. Could a person match the light's speed in order to observe it? This question would one day drive Albert to the theory that changed the field of physics forever.

Meanwhile, Albert's life was changing in drastic ways. His father's business was struggling again, and money was tight. In 1894 the family left Munich and moved to Italy without Albert. Albert moved in with a distant relative so he could complete his studies in Munich.

For months, Albert was miserable. He blamed growing anti-Semitism in Germany for his father's business failing. He also knew that if he stayed in Germany, the law would force him, as a boy over sixteen, to serve in the German army. After enduring six months, Albert withdrew from school without his parents' permission. He traveled to Italy to reunite with his family. But the reunion was brief. Albert needed to continue his education, and he did not speak Italian. He soon moved on to Zurich, Switzerland.

Anti-Semitism in Germany

Anti-Semitism is prejudice against Jewish people. As a teenager, Albert observed growing anti-Semitism in Germany. The prejudice disturbed and frightened him. Anti-Semitism had always existed in Germany and elsewhere. But by the 1890s, it had grown worse. Many Germans wrongly blamed Jewish people for Germany's financial problems. Albert feared that this prejudice would make life difficult for Jewish people living there. His fears played a large role in his decision to leave Germany and eventually renounce, or abandon, his German citizenship.

Into Adulthood

Life in Zurich was happier for Albert. He enrolled in school and continued to study math and physics. His new school was very different from the one in Germany. Teachers did not drill students. Instead, they guided them and encouraged them to learn on their own. The looser teaching style gave Albert the freedom of thought and expression he had always wanted. He passed his exams and moved on to college at the Swiss Federal Polytechnic School.

There, Albert continued to thrive. His grades improved, and he grew more social and outgoing. He became friends with another student, Mileva Maric, who shared his love of math and science. Soon their friendship blossomed into a

The main building of the Swiss Federal Polytechnic School in Zurich, where Einstein attended college

Einstein at his desk in the patent office

romance. Albert admired her intelligence and her drive to succeed. The pair studied together, and some speculate that Mileva may even have contributed to Albert's early work. However, because of her Serbian heritage and Christian faith, Albert's father did not approve of the match.

Einstein finished his studies at the Swiss Federal Polytechnic School in 1900 and earned a teaching diploma. That year he published his first paper in a major scientific journal. He began to search for a teaching job but had trouble finding a permanent one. For income, he took the job in the patent office. Inventors applied for patents to protect the rights to sell their inventions.

Mileva Maric, Einstein's first wife, with their two sons, Hans (*right*) and Eduard (*left*)

Though the job did not excite him, some of the inventions he reviewed sparked his mind.

Meanwhile, Einstein's romance with Maric continued, despite his father's objections. In 1902 Maric gave birth to a daughter, Lieserl. Einstein and Maric weren't married at the time of Lieserl's birth. Births outside of marriage were frowned on at the time, so the couple kept her arrival a secret. No one knows what happened to the child. Some believe Maric gave her up for adoption. Others think she died as an infant. Einstein and Maric married a year later and went on to have two more children: Hans, born in 1904, and Eduard, born in 1910.

The Miracle Year

In 1905 Einstein earned his PhD from the University of Zurich. It marked the start of what some would later call his miracle year. Einstein had never stopped thinking about the workings of the universe, especially those related to light. The image of speeding alongside a beam of light continued to intrigue him. The more he thought about it, the more he realized that the universe must work in ways no one had ever imagined.

Einstein's insights came in waves. Over a few months, he published four scientific papers. The first two dealt

Annalen der Physik, or *Annals of Physics*, the journal in which Einstein published his papers for other scientists to read and discuss

with how the tiniest bits of matter move. They also explored how heat affects this movement. But those papers' impact was small compared to what followed.

In the third paper, Einstein challenged the standing theory of what light was. At the time, most scientists agreed that light was a wave. But Einstein showed that this simple definition was impossible. Light, he concluded, must be composed of particles.

Einstein's theory showed the dual nature of light. It was a strange idea that meant light could act as both

Light behaves strangely in many situations. In prisms, it makes reflections appear to twist and bend.

a wave and as a particle. The paper turned the physics world upside down. Einstein explained that light could be broken down into its tiniest form, quanta. This meant there must be a whole quantum universe—a world of particles smaller than an atom. The revelation kicked off an entire new branch of science called quantum physics. Researchers in the new field set out to describe the world of these tiny particles.

For an ordinary physicist, the paper would have been the achievement of a lifetime. But Einstein wasn't done. His next paper introduced a theory called special relativity.

Special relativity said that the speed of light was always the same. It did not depend on the movement or viewpoint of an observer. So an observer standing still and an observer in motion would both see light traveling at the same speed. Their motion or lack thereof would not affect how they saw moving light.

To many, this seemed to go against common sense. They compared light to other moving objects such as horses or cars. To an observer on the side of the road, cars seem to move very quickly. To an observer riding in a car, other cars seem to move slowly. Einstein was claiming that light speed was constant no matter what.

The implications of the theory were very strange. If the speed of light was the same no matter the observer, then objects moving at different speeds experienced time differently. As an observer accelerated at a speed closer and closer to the speed of light, time would pass more and more slowly. If an observer could ever reach the speed of light, time would stop altogether! Einstein's theory showed that time and space were far more bizarre—and connected—than anyone had previously thought.

"I sometimes ask myself how it came about that I was the one to develop the theory of relativity," Einstein later wrote. "The reason, I think, is that a normal adult never stops to think about problems of space and time. These are things which he has thought of as a child. But my intellectual development was [slow], as a result of which I began to wonder about space and time only when I had already grown up."

In November of that year, Einstein published a fifth paper—the one for which he is most famous. It introduced the idea of mass-energy equivalence. Einstein showed that mass and energy were made of the same material. To explain the relationship between them, he created an equation: $E=mc^2$. The equation states that energy equals mass times the speed of light squared, or multiplied by itself.

The equation could calculate the amount of energy mass contained. Though Einstein could not have known it at the time, this calculation would form the basis for the most powerful weapon ever built just four decades later.

Once again, Einstein had forever changed physics. His miracle year saw him publish a flurry of new and groundbreaking ideas, and Einstein became a worldwide celebrity almost overnight. Science would never be the same, and neither would Einstein's life.

Relativity Revised

By 1908 Einstein was a lecturer at the University of Bern in Switzerland. In 1909 he accepted a position as an associate professor at the University of Zurich. Two years later, he became a full professor at the University of Prague. He published papers on topics such as quantum theory and radiation.

Meanwhile, Einstein continued to think about special relativity. The gaps in his theory troubled him. Special relativity applied only in a universe that was flat. The theory did not account for gravity, which curves the fabric of space-time. Feeling his theory was incomplete, Einstein set out to find a way to account for gravity.

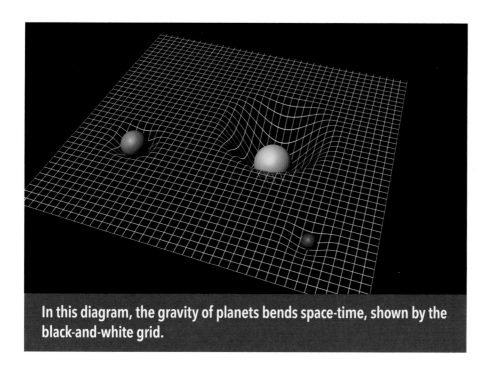

In this diagram, the gravity of planets bends space-time, shown by the black-and-white grid.

Scientists had to wait for the eclipse to test general relativity. Ordinarily, the sun's light was too bright to see the light from other stars.

Beginning in 1911, he published papers expanding on special relativity.

Finally, in 1915, Einstein published a new but related theory: general relativity. General relativity filled in many of the gaps in his theory of special relativity. Einstein described gravity as a bending of space itself. Einstein theorized that according to general relativity, the gravity of the sun should bend the light of a distant star. Suddenly, relativity was more than just ideas and mathematics. For the first time, scientists could test it.

Four years later, two groups of scientists on opposite sides of the globe observed a solar eclipse. During a solar eclipse, the moon passes in front of the sun, blocking its light. The scientists took careful measurements of light from distant stars as the moon traveled past the eclipsed sun. Their results showed the sun's gravity was indeed bending the light of the stars that passed behind it. Most scientists agreed that the results proved Einstein's theory correct.

Einstein's Biggest Blunder?

Einstein believed that the universe was static, or unchanging. He did not think it was getting bigger or smaller. But his theory of general relativity meant that gravity should be pulling the universe together.

If the universe was static, as Einstein believed, then an invisible force must be canceling out the pull of gravity. This force must be pushing outward with the same force that gravity pulls inward. Einstein called the outward force the cosmological constant. Many physicists agreed that the cosmological constant had to exist. But in 1929, astronomer Edwin Hubble observed that the universe was expanding. Einstein had been wrong.

The Hubble Space Telescope is named after Edwin Hubble for his contributions to astronomy.

The universe was not static. Einstein called the idea of the constant his biggest blunder.

A century later, physicists believe that Einstein's cosmological constant is real. A force they call dark energy appears to be pushing the universe to expand far more quickly than gravity can cause it to contract. Einstein's cosmological constant was not his biggest blunder. Even when he was wrong, he was right.

Einstein's theory gave physicists a new way to study the universe. It also predicted some wild and amazing things. According to general relativity, there must exist gravity fields powerful enough to prevent even light from escaping. These fields were black holes. Though scientists proved the existence of black holes years later, the idea of them was so strange that even Einstein had trouble believing they were real.

Einstein was moving science forward in giant leaps. He was more famous than ever, and his career was soaring. Meanwhile, his private life was in turmoil. He had fallen in love with Elsa Löwenthal, his first cousin. His love for Löwenthal drove a wedge between him and his wife. They finally divorced in 1919. Soon after, Einstein married Löwenthal and adopted her two daughters, Margot and Ilse.

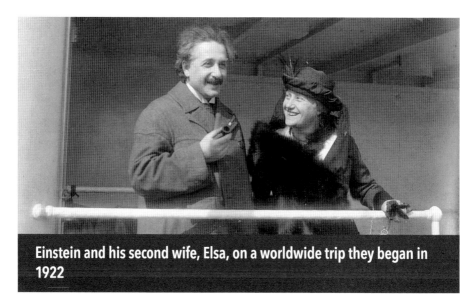

Einstein and his second wife, Elsa, on a worldwide trip they began in 1922

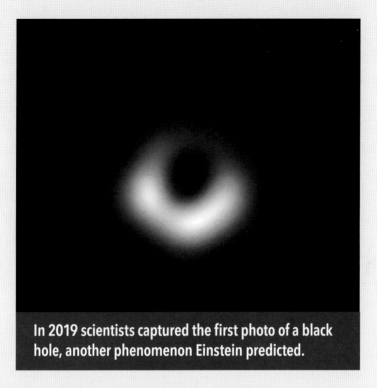
In 2019 scientists captured the first photo of a black hole, another phenomenon Einstein predicted.

A Century ahead of His Time

In 1916 Einstein predicted the existence of gravitational waves. He explained that these waves would be ripples in space-time created by large, accelerating masses. At the time, there was no way to prove or disprove Einstein's idea. For almost one hundred years, gravitational waves remained only a theory.

In 2015 scientists found evidence of the phenomena Einstein had predicted. Their high-tech equipment detected gravitational waves for the first time. Scientists believe that a collision between two black holes created the waves.

Travels and Turmoil

In 1921 Einstein was awarded the Nobel Prize in Physics. In 1922 he embarked on a long tour of the world. He traveled to many places, including Japan, Egypt, and Palestine, the ancestral home of the Jewish people. Einstein was welcomed as a hero wherever he went. People flocked to hear him speak.

As Einstein continued his travels, he became a symbol for both science and international cooperation. Over the next decade, he served intermittently on the International Committee on Intellectual Cooperation of the League of Nations. The committee's goal was to encourage knowledge sharing between scientists, researchers, teachers, and artists around the globe.

While other scientists focused on better understanding relativity, Einstein turned to other mysteries. The shift

Albert (*right*) and Elsa Einstein in Japan in 1922

Playing Dice

Einstein struggled with the strange properties of the quantum universe. At the smallest scales of space and time, particles can appear and disappear. They can be in two places at the same time. Much of their behavior seems driven by randomness.

Einstein rejected the idea that randomness, rather than cause and effect, could play such a major role in driving reality. In a 1926 letter, he wrote, "God does not play dice with the universe." It became one of his most famous quotes. However, it is often misunderstood. Some people think the quote shows Einstein believed in both God and destiny. He did not believe in either. He was simply trying to say that he believed events in the universe had causes.

came partly because of the difficult math involved in describing relativity. Einstein admitted that much of the math was beyond him. He had developed relativity largely out of thought experiments, not mathematics. "Since the mathematicians have invaded the theory of relativity, I do not understand it myself anymore," he said.

Instead, Einstein began to search for a unified field theory. His goal was to find a theory that united the four known universal forces: weak nuclear, strong nuclear, gravitational, and electromagnetic. Almost a century later, the problem remains unsolved.

In 1930 Einstein traveled to the United States. In a whirlwind tour of the country, he and his wife met with reporters, top US scientists, famous actors, writers, and more. They were even special guests of actor Charlie Chaplin at the premiere of his new film, *City Lights*. Einstein and Chaplin became lifelong friends.

Einstein returned to Germany after his trip. But he did not stay long. The nation had been struggling since losing World War I (1914–1918). Its economy was in shambles, and nationalism was on the rise. The Nazi Party took advantage of the situation. It spread propaganda claiming Germans were a superior race of people. The Nazis blamed other races, especially Jews, for Germany's struggles.

Adolf Hitler was at the center of the Nazi movement. In speeches, Hitler promised to restore Germany to its former glory. Meanwhile, Einstein grew increasingly worried by the shift toward bigotry in his home country. The German

The Einsteins with actor Charlie Chaplin at the *City Lights* premiere

Paul von Hindenburg (*right*) appointed Hitler chancellor, after which Hitler began to take total control of the German government.

government began targeting Jewish people with harsh, unfair laws. Einstein's standing in the global community made him a special target. The Nazis burned his books and hired physicists to prove his theories wrong. As the Nazis grew in power, Einstein believed his life was in danger.

In 1933 Hitler became chancellor of Germany. Einstein believed that the country had reached a tipping point. Germany was no longer safe for him or for anyone of Jewish heritage. It was time to leave.

World Affairs

In 1933 Einstein joined the many Jewish scientists fleeing Germany. He traveled to the United States, where he was briefly a professor at California Institute of Technology. From there, he sailed to Belgium.

Later that year, Einstein met with Winston Churchill, soon to be the prime minister of Britain. Einstein warned Churchill of the dangers to Jewish scientists in Germany. He begged Churchill to help bring them safely out of the country. Churchill agreed to take measures to help scientists escape. Afterward, Einstein continued to travel to ask other world leaders for help. The world was only just beginning to realize the dangers that Nazi Germany presented. Einstein was a powerful voice in spreading that message.

In October 1933, Einstein returned to the United States. He took a position at the Institute for Advanced Study in Princeton, New Jersey. It was a dark time in Einstein's personal life. His son Eduard was struggling with mental illness and living in an institution. Elsa Einstein's health

After Einstein's visit, Churchill (*left*) helped Jewish scientists flee Germany and find work at British universities.

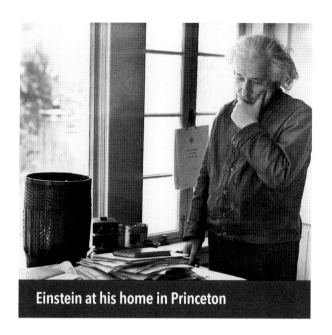
Einstein at his home in Princeton

was also declining. She died in 1936. Meanwhile, events in Europe grew more troubling. Einstein was a pacifist. He hated war. But it seemed more and more certain that his homeland would start one.

World War II (1939–1945) broke out when Germany invaded Poland. Scientists in other parts of Europe were increasingly alarmed about the Nazi threat. Among them was physicist Leó Szilárd. Szilárd understood that Einstein's famous equation, $E=mc^2$, meant that small amounts of matter could unleash massive amounts of energy. He feared that Germany would use that knowledge to build a weapon of terrible power: an atomic bomb.

In 1939 Szilárd wrote a letter to US president Franklin D. Roosevelt. The letter warned Roosevelt of the danger of atomic weapons. Szilárd urged the United States to begin its own research to create them. Einstein cosigned the letter. Perhaps due to Einstein's support,

Roosevelt took the threat seriously. He started the Manhattan Project to build an atomic bomb.

Einstein felt extremely conflicted. As a pacifist, he was against war in any form. Urging the United States to build the most powerful weapon ever created flew in the face of his beliefs. But Einstein was certain that if Germany developed the bomb first, disaster would follow. The outcome would be better, he reasoned, if the United States beat Germany to it.

The Manhattan Project succeeded. The United States created two types of atomic bombs, both of them hugely powerful. The fighting in Europe was over by the time the bombs were ready. But in the Pacific Ocean, the war raged on between the US and Japan. In August 1945, the US dropped the bombs on two Japanese cities, Hiroshima and

Roosevelt gives an address in 1939, the year World War II began.

On July 16, 1945, researchers successfully detonated the first atomic bomb at a secret site in New Mexico.

Nagasaki. The bombs destroyed the cities and killed over two hundred thousand people. Japan had to surrender.

World War II was over. But Einstein never forgave himself for helping to convince the United States to develop atomic weapons. He called it the one great mistake of his life.

Speaking Out

By the 1940s, Einstein was the world's most famous scientist. Yet he had turned much of his attention to social causes and justice. Einstein believed that any person could succeed in the United States. But he saw one glaring flaw in its culture: racism. Some historians believe Einstein compared the treatment of black people in the United States to the treatment of Jews in Nazi Germany.

Einstein joined the National Association for the Advancement of Colored People (NAACP) in Princeton. He spoke out publicly against racism. "There is separation of colored people from white people in the United States," Einstein said. "That separation is not a disease of colored people. It is a disease of white people. I do not intend to be quiet about it."

One of Einstein's biggest concerns was lynching. Lynching is execution, often by hanging, without due process. Einstein was the cochair of the American Crusade Against Lynching. He spoke to US president Harry Truman to seek laws to protect black Americans against lynching.

Einstein and others demanded that Truman announce the government's opposition to lynching and punish those who partook in it.

W. E. B. DuBois in 1950

Einstein befriended leaders in the black community. One of them was civil rights leader W. E. B. DuBois. In 1951 the US government accused DuBois of acting as a foreign agent. Einstein volunteered to speak as a character witness for DuBois. Einstein was incredibly popular and well respected. Possibly because of his intervention, the government dropped the charges.

In 1948 the United Nations helped to create the independent state of Israel for the Jewish people. When its first president, Chaim Weizmann, died in 1952, Israel's leaders offered Einstein the presidency. Then seventy-three years old, Einstein turned it down. He said he was

Einstein (*center left*) with Chaim Weizmann (*center right*), the future president of Israel, and other Jewish leaders in 1921

too old, too inexperienced, and lacked the social skills needed for the job. But the offer showed the great respect the Jewish people had for him.

Death and Legacy

Einstein's time as a productive scientist was behind him. He lived out his days in Princeton. For his seventy-fifth birthday, Einstein received a parrot as a gift. He passed time by telling the parrot bad jokes. He faked illnesses to get out of seeing an endless stream of visitors. He wrote poetry and went sailing.

In the late 1940s, Einstein had developed an aneurysm, or a bulge in a blood vessel. He had surgery to fix it temporarily. But in April 1955, his condition again began to worsen. This time, he refused surgery. "It is tasteless to prolong life artificially," he said. "I have done my share. It is time to go. I will do it elegantly."

In the hospital dying, Einstein continued to work. He jotted down equations. He spoke to friends and fellow

Einstein enjoyed sailing in his later years, though he never learned how to swim.

Einstein in 1954, just before he turned seventy-five

scientists. He worked on a speech he was to give on Israel's Independence Day.

On April 18, Einstein's nurse heard him say something in German, although she could not understand what he had said. They were Einstein's final words. Einstein was dead. He was seventy-six years old.

Doctors did an autopsy to learn the cause of Einstein's death. During the autopsy, one of them took his brain and preserved it without the permission of Einstein's family.

Scientists studied Einstein's brain, hoping to find the key to his genius. They found some small differences, but nothing that could explain Einstein's ability to see the universe in a unique way.

Einstein had no funeral. He was cremated soon after the autopsy. His ashes were scattered on the grounds of Princeton's Institute for Advanced Study.

After his death, Einstein remained a symbol of scientific achievement. His name alone came to mean "genius." His contributions, personality, and wild hair made him a cultural icon. In 1999 *Time* named him Person of the Century. The magazine called him the most important scientist in a century filled with scientific advancements.

Einstein was far ahead of his time. His insights still form the basis of the modern understanding of time and space. From a child who a teacher once said would never amount to anything, Einstein grew into perhaps the brightest mind the world has ever known.

IMPORTANT DATES

1879   Albert Einstein is born on March 14 in Ulm, in the German Empire.

1884   He begins attending Catholic school in Munich, Germany. He struggles in school.

1894   The Einstein family leaves Munich, leaving Albert behind to complete his education.

1895   Einstein moves to Zurich to continue his education.

1900   He publishes his first scientific paper.

1903   He marries Mileva Maric.

1905   He publishes a flurry of papers that overturn much of classical physics.

1911   He becomes a full professor at the University of Prague.

1915   He publishes his general theory of relativity.

1919   He divorces Mileva and marries Elsa Löwenthal.

1921	He is awarded the Nobel Prize in Physics.
1933	He flees Germany, fearing the Nazi Party's persecution of Jews.
1939	World War II begins. Einstein cosigns a letter to US president Franklin Delano Roosevelt urging the United States to develop atomic weapons.
1952	Israel offers Einstein its presidency. He declines.
1955	On April 18, Einstein dies of a burst aneurysm.
2015	Scientists confirm the existence of gravitational waves, which Einstein predicted ninety-nine years earlier.

SOURCE NOTES

11 Alice Calaprice and Trevor Lipscombe, *Albert Einstein: A Biography* (Westport, CT: Greenwood, 2005), 3.

22 Richard Rhodes, *The Making of the Atomic Bomb* (New York: Simon & Schuster, 1986), 172.

29 P. A. Schilpp, *Albert Einstein, Philosopher-Scientist* (La Salle, IL: Open Court, 2000), 102.

29 Kelly Dickerson, "One of Einstein's Most Famous Quotes Is Often Completely Misinterpreted," Business Insider, November 19, 2015, https://www.businessinsider.com/god-does-not-play-dice -quote-meaning-2015-11.

36 Matthew Francis, "How Albert Einstein Used His Fame to Denounce American Racism," *Smithsonian*, March 3, 2017, https://www.smithsonianmag.com/science-nature/how-celebrity -scientist-albert-einstein-used-fame-denounce-american -racism-180962356/.

39 Walter Isaacson, *Einstein: His Life and Universe* (London: Pocket Books, 2007), 542.

SELECTED BIBLIOGRAPHY

Associated Press. "Diary Sheds Light on Einstein's Final Years." *NBC News*, April 26, 2004. http://www.nbcnews.com/id/4829521/ns /technology_and_science-science/t/diary-sheds-light-einsteins -final-years/#.XNnCE45Ki70.

Calaprice, Alice, and Trevor Lipscombe. *Albert Einstein: A Biography*. Westport, CT: Greenwood, 2005.

Cosgrove, Ben. "The Day Albert Einstein Died: A Photographer's Story." *Time*. Last modified March 17, 2016. http://time.com/3494553 /the-day-albert-einstein-died-a-photographers-story/.

Gimbel, Steven. *Einstein: His Space and Times*. New Haven, CT: Yale University Press, 2015.

Harris, Richard. "Albert Einstein's Year of Miracles: Light Theory." *National Public Radio*, March 17, 2005. https://www.npr.org /2005/03/17/4538324/albert-einsteins-year-of-miracles-light-theory.

Lerner, Aaron B. *Einstein & Newton: A Comparison of the Two Greatest Scientists*. Minneapolis: Lerner Publications, 1973.

Panek, Richard. "The Year of Albert Einstein." *Smithsonian*, June 2005. https://www.smithsonianmag.com/science-nature/the-year-of-albert -einstein-75841381/.

Rhodes, Richard. *The Making of the Atomic Bomb*. New York: Simon & Schuster, 1986.

Schilpp, P. A. *Albert Einstein, Philosopher-Scientist*. La Salle, IL: Open Court, 2000.

FURTHER READING

BOOKS

Bayarri, Jordi. *Albert Einstein and the Theory of Relativity*. Minneapolis: Graphic Universe, 2020.
This graphic biography traces Einstein's life, career, and travels.

Gaughan, Richard. *Physics in Your Everyday Life*. New York: Enslow, 2020.
What is physics? What role does it play in daily life? Learn about light, electricity, states of matter, and more.

Marsico, Katie. *Genius Physicist Albert Einstein*. Minneapolis: Lerner Publications, 2018.
Follow the events of Einstein's life, from his struggles in school to the discoveries that changed science forever.

WEBSITES

Ducksters: Theory of Relativity
https://www.ducksters.com/science/physics/theory_of_relativity.php
What is relativity? How does it work? Learn more about what Einstein's theory means.

Einstein Museum
https://www.bern.com/en/detail/einstein-museum
Learn more about the brilliant physicist's life and career at the website of the Einstein Museum in Bern, Switzerland.

Khan Academy: Introduction to Physics
https://www.khanacademy.org/science/physics/one-dimensional
-motion/introduction-to-physics-tutorial/v/introduction-to-physics
This video explains the basics of physics and its relationship to the world.

INDEX